American Lives

Buzz Aldrin

Elizabeth Raum

Heinemann Library
Chicago, Illinois

Designed by Joanna Hinton-Malivoire and
Q2A Creative

Printed in China by
WKT Company Limited

10 09 08 07 06
10 9 8 7 6 5 4 3 2 1

Library of Congress Cataloging-in-Publication Data
Raum, Elizabeth.
  Buzz Aldrin / Elizabeth Raum.
    p. cm. -- (American lives)
  Includes bibliographical references and index.
  ISBN 1-4034-6939-3 (hc) -- ISBN 1-4034-6946-6
(pb)
 1. Aldrin, Buzz--Juvenile literature. 2. Astronauts--
United States--Biography--Juvenile literature. 3.
Space flight to the moon--Juvenile literature. 4.
Project Apollo (U.S.)--Juvenile literature.
I. Title. II. Series.
  TL789.85.A4R38 2005
  629.45'0092--dc22

                    2005006249

Acknowledgments
The author and publishers are grateful to the
following for permission to reproduce copyright
material: Alamy Images p. 14 (Michael Dwyer);
BuzzAldrin.com pp. 5, 8, 10; Corbis pp. 9 (Ted
Speigel), 23; Corbis/Bettmann cover, title page, pp.
6, 12, 16, 21, 27; Corbis/NASA p. 25; Corbis/Reuters
pp. 28, 29; Getty Images/Time-Life Pictures p. 7;
NASA pp. 4, 24; NASA/Johnson Space Center pp.
15, 17, 18, 20; NASA/Kennedy Space Center pp. 22,
26; NASA/Marshall Space Flight Center p. 19;
Topham Picturepoint p. 13

Every effort has been made to contact copyright
holders of any material reproduced in this book.
Any omissions will be rectified in subsequent
printings if notice is given to the publisher.

The photograph on the cover is the official NASA
portrait of Buzz Aldrin, taken in 1966.

Contents

Some words are shown in bold, **like this.** You can find out what they mean by looking in the glossary.

Buzz

Buzz Aldrin walked on the Moon. He also jogged and hopped like a kangaroo. But he found it worked best to gallop the way a child does when imitating a horse. Buzz reported that stepping on the Moon was like stepping into powder. When he put his foot down, the powder settled around it, and the footprints remained. On July 20, 1969, Neil Armstrong and Buzz Aldrin were the first people to leave their marks on the Moon.

Buzz Aldrin left his mark, a footprint, on the moon. It is still visible today.

Timeline

1930	1954	1964	1966	1971
Born on January 20 in Montclair, New Jersey	Marries Joan Archer	Begins astronaut training; Lands on Moon, Apollo 11	Goes into space on Gemini 12	Works as professor at University of Cincinnati

Buzz is shown here with his parents and his sisters Madeline and Fay Ann.

Edwin Eugene Aldrin, Jr. was born on January 20, 1930, in Montclair, New Jersey. His sister Madeline was four years older. Fay Ann, who was only a year and a half old, tried to call the new baby *Brother*. It came out *buzzer*. The name stuck. Buzz's father was a pilot and he knew of Charles Lindbergh and Amelia Earhart, who were both famous pilots. His mother's maiden name was Marion Moon.

1973	1988	1998	2000	2005
Publishes **autobiography**, Return to Earth	*Marries Lois Driggs*	*Begins ShareSpace Foundation*	*Publishes* The Return, *a science fiction novel*	*Writes autobiography for children*

Childhood

Buzz's family lived in Montclair, New Jersey. Buzz was only two years old when his father took him up in a Lockhead Vega airplane painted like an eagle. Buzz loved flying, even though his first flight made him sick. Buzz was small and wiry when he was a boy, but he was full of energy. He loved peanut butter sandwiches with sliced bananas and topped with chocolate. He ate tuna out of the can and dry Jell-O.

At age two, Buzz plays with his model ship during a vacation in Florida.

Buzz enjoyed playing football more than he liked studying. His favorite sports were tumbling and pole-vaulting. He spent hours practicing in the backyard. One summer, Buzz discovered scuba diving. He was fascinated. When he became an astronaut, his scuba diving skills helped him prepare for walking in space.

When he was an astronaut, Buzz still enjoyed pole-vaulting.

West Point

When Buzz began high school, he realized that he would need good grades to get into West Point, a military academy in New York. He played football for Montclair High School, but he also spent his time studying. His grades were good. He was **admitted** to West Point. Buzz entered West Point on July 1, 1947.

This picture shows Buzz as a student at West Point.

West Point

West Point is a college run by the Army. When they graduate, students must serve five years in the Army or Air Force. They become Second Lieutenants.

West Point, located 55 miles (89 km) north of New York City, has been training Army officers since 1802.

Sports are also important at West Point. Buzz took part in pole-vaulting. Even though he was small and wiry, Buzz was a good athlete. His best vault was 13 feet 9 inches.

Buzz spent four years at West Point studying and preparing for life in the Army. He **graduated** third in his class. He had already decided to enter the Air Force and become a fighter pilot.

Pilot

Buzz is shown here climbing into a fighter plane.

Aldrin headed to Bartow, Florida, to learn how to fly planes. He spent six months in Florida training to be a fighter pilot. He then moved to Nellis Air Force Base in Nevada. The Korean War had begun, and the Air Force needed pilots.

Korean War

The Korean War (1950–1953) was between North and South Korea. The United States was fighting with the South Koreans against the North Koreans.

Aldrin arrived in Korea in December 1952. He spent the first weeks training to fly **combat** missions. In February, he joined the fighting. He flew in 66 combat missions and shot down 2 Korean fighter planes. He won the Distinguished Flying Cross for his courage and bravery. Aldrin returned to his home in New Jersey in 1952.

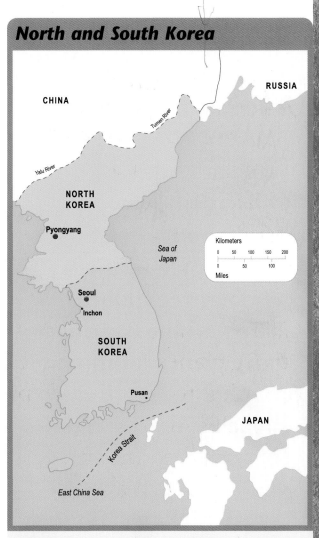

North and South Korea

This map shows the area where the Korean War took place.

Air Force Life

While he was home, Aldrin began dating a young woman named Joan Archer. The Air Force sent Aldrin to Nevada to train pilots, so he and Joan decided to write to each other. They soon realized that they loved one another.

On December 29, 1954, they married. The Aldrins moved to Alabama so that Buzz could attend Squadron Officer School where he learned how to be a leader. He finished school three months later, and the Aldrins moved to Colorado.

Joan Archer became Mrs. Buzz Aldrin when they married in 1954.

This picture, taken in the 1960s, shows Aldrin with his wife and three children.

The Aldrins settled into their Colorado home. Buzz worked at the Air Force Academy training pilots. In September 1955, their first son, James Michael, was born. Buzz, now called Captain Aldrin, was eager to return to flying. He moved to Bitburg, Germany, to join the 36th Fighter Day Wing. He learned to fly fast planes called F-100s. By the time the Aldrins left Germany in 1959, two more children, Janice and Andy, had been born.

MIT

MIT is located in Cambridge, Massachusetts, near Boston.

Captain Aldrin faced an important decision. He wanted to be an astronaut, but all the men chosen to be Mercury astronauts had been test pilots. Should he go to test pilot school? Aldrin knew that getting more education would be important in future space missions, so he decided to go to the Massachusetts Institute of Technology (MIT) to get a doctor of science degree. He wanted to study a problem that would make him helpful to space flight.

Aldrin chose to study the problem of **rendezvous**, the joining together of two vehicles in space. Computers would help to control space rendezvous, but Aldrin knew that if the computers failed, then the astronauts would need to know how to take over. Aldrin's study proved important to future trips into space. When **NASA** announced they were looking for astronauts, Aldrin applied.

In this picture, the Agena rocket prepares to dock, or rendezvous, with the *Gemini* space capsule.

Astronaut

Aldrin was in the third group of astronauts. On October 17, 1963, **NASA** announced that Buzz Aldrin was one of fourteen new astronauts. In January 1964, he reported to the Manned Spacecraft Center in Houston and began training.

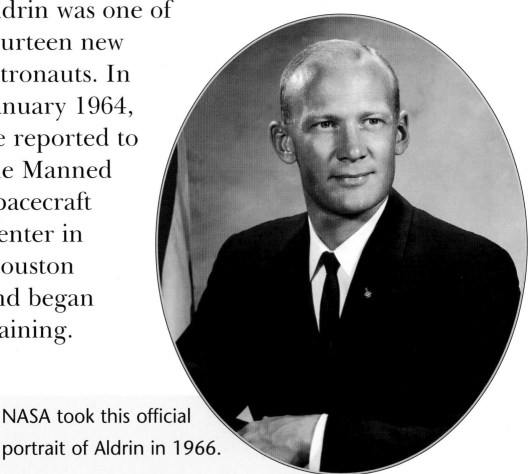

NASA took this official portrait of Aldrin in 1966.

Group Three

The first group, of seven astronauts, were called Mercury astronauts. The second nine were called the Gemini astronauts. Aldrin's group of fourteen were called the Group Three astronauts. They flew both Gemini and Apollo missions.

Aldrin is seated in the front row, left, in this photograph of Group Three Astronauts.

The **goal** of the space program was a Moon landing. Each astronaut worked on what he knew best. While he waited to be **assigned** to a space flight, Aldrin worked on plans and **procedures** for two spacecraft to meet and connect in space. The other astronauts called Aldrin Dr. **Rendezvous** because of his work at MIT and his interest in planning for the perfect rendezvous.

Gemini 12

In 1966, Aldrin was **assigned** as back-up for *Gemini 9* pilot Eugene Cernan. Aldrin and Cernan practiced for hours. The mission would include a space walk. When Aldrin heard an astronaut say that walking in space was like walking under water, he began training in a swimming pool. He wore a special space suit so that he could breathe easily and practice the jobs he would do in space. His first space flight, *Gemini 12*, included a space walk. James Lovell was the co-pilot with Aldrin.

This is an actual photograph of Aldrin walking in space and working on the Agena rocket.

This picture shows the launch of the Atlas-Agena booster carrying the target vehicle for the *Gemini 12* mission on November 11, 1966.

Gemini 12 lifted off on November 11, 1966. Aldrin suited up and stepped out of the space **capsule**. During his first space walk he took pictures of **constellations**. During his second, the longest one, he repaired the Agena rocket. When he looked down, he realized that he was 160 miles (257 kilometers) above the Earth. He was not afraid. Walking in space was just like walking under water. On his third walk, he took more pictures. The space walk was a great success.

Preparing for Moon Landing

Gemini 12 splashed down in the Atlantic Ocean four days after blast-off. It was the last Gemini flight. Aldrin and Lovell went to visit President Lyndon Johnson at his Texas ranch. Then they went to New York and Washington, D.C., for more celebrations.

NASA scientists and astronauts used the information from the Gemini flights to plan for a Moon landing. The **goal** of the Apollo program was to send three men to the Moon.

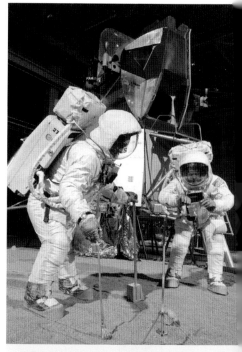

This photo shows Aldrin practicing using tongs to pick up a sample of Moon rock.

Buzz Aldrin Firsts

Buzz Aldrin was the first person to:

- *make three space walks on a single mission*
- *pilot a **lunar module** to a landing on the Moon*

The astronauts began training for the Moon landing. They trained in **simulators**, machines made to act like space vehicles. They traveled to Hawaii, Idaho, Oregon, and Iceland to study rock **formations** like those they might find on the Moon. Aldrin also learned to fly a helicopter. Flying helicopters taught astronauts how to fly the lunar lander. Aldrin knew that he might be the one to fly the lunar lander to the Moon's surface.

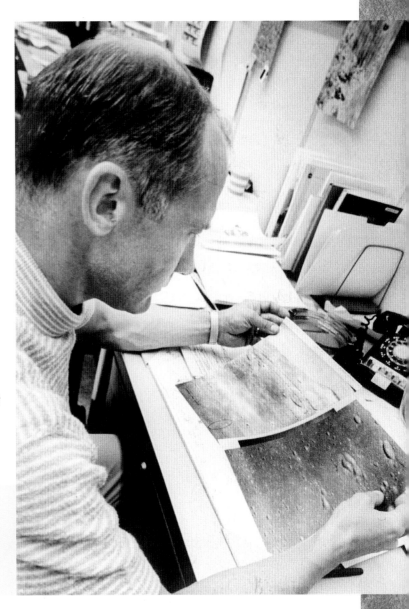

Aldrin studies charts of possible Moon landing sites.

Flying to the Moon

On January 6, 1969, Aldrin was assigned to *Apollo 11*. He was going to the Moon! Neil Armstrong would be the commander and Michael Collins would pilot *Columbia*, the **command module**. Aldrin's job was to pilot *Eagle*, the **lunar module**. All three astronauts worked nonstop to get ready for the flight.

At 9:32 a.m. on July 16, 1969, *Apollo 11* blasted into space. Millions of Americans watched on television as the astronauts headed to the Moon.

Apollo 11 lifts off from the Kennedy Space Center in Florida.

The astronauts got a good view of the Moon craters, like this one, as they passed overhead.

It took the *Columbia* three days to reach **orbit** around the Moon. Armstrong and Aldrin floated into the *Eagle*, turned on the computers, and checked the systems. They put on their space suits and prepared to separate from the *Columbia*. The *Eagle* pulled away from *Columbia* with Aldrin and Armstrong inside. Michael Collins remained in *Columbia* orbiting the Moon. Armstrong and Aldrin watched the Moon getting closer and closer. Finally, they landed on the Moon's surface.

Bouncing on the Moon

Neil Armstrong took this picture of Aldrin walking on the Moon.

Aldrin and Armstrong were eager to step onto the Moon, but first Aldrin took a moment to thank God for their safe arrival. He asked everyone listening on their radios or television to join him in giving thanks. Then the astronauts put on their space suits and prepared to step onto the Moon. Armstrong would go first because he was nearest the door. Aldrin would follow. He waited in the **capsule**, guiding Armstrong down the steps of the **lunar module**.

Armstrong and Aldrin took pictures of the Moon and of each other. Then they set up experiments so that scientists could learn about the Moon. They collected Moon rocks. Finally, they placed a United States flag on the Moon. Much of what they did was captured on camera and sent back to people on Earth. All too soon it was time to get back into the lunar module and **dock** with *Columbia*.

Astronaut Buzz Aldrin approaches the leg of the *Eagle*.

Fame

Aldrin had no trouble docking the *Eagle* with *Columbia*. His work on **rendezvous** had paid off. Four days later, *Apollo 11* splashed down in the Pacific Ocean. Because scientists feared that the astronauts might have picked up some germs on the Moon, they were kept **isolated** from other people for eighteen days. No one got sick, and in August 1969, they returned to their families. They were national heroes.

The astronauts waited for rescue after splashdown.

New York City welcomed the astronauts with a parade. Aldrin is sitting between astronauts Collins and Armstrong.

Buzz and his family were surprised by the attention. Reporters camped on their lawn. **NASA** sent the astronauts and their wives on a tour of the United States and a tour of the world. Montclair, New Jersey, had a special celebration for Buzz Aldrin. The astronauts were awarded Presidential Medals of Freedom and spoke to Congress. At first the astronauts enjoyed the attention, but it soon became tiring. Aldrin wondered if he would ever live a normal life again.

Writer and Dreamer

In 1971 Aldrin **retired** from **NASA**. Soon afterwards, he retired from the Air Force. In 1973, he wrote his **autobiography**, *Return to Earth*. In it he talks about his space flights and his struggle with **depression**, an illness that made him feel discouraged. His marriage to Joan ended, and in 1988, he married Lois Driggs. The next year he wrote *Men from Earth* about his trip to the Moon.

Aldrin looks at a G.I. Joe figure made to look like him in 1999.

In 1993 Aldrin designed a new space station. He also **founded** a company called Starcraft Boosters, Inc. to design rockets. He imagines a time when ordinary people can travel to the Moon, to Mars, and beyond.

In 1996 and 2000, he wrote science fiction novels, and in 2005 he wrote a children's book about his life. Although Buzz Aldrin has received many medals and awards for his scientific work, nothing can match the excitement he felt as he bounced on the Moon.

On July 20, 1999, Aldrin (right), Armstrong (middle), and Collins (left) received medals to honor the *Apollo 11* Moon landing.

Glossary

admit   accept into a school or program

announce   tell

assign   appoint

autobiography   story of one's own life

capsule   closed space designed to protect a person

combat   battle

command module   main part of the spaceship carrying the astronauts

constellation   group of stars

depression   sadness; a feeling of discouragement

dock   meet or connect

formation   group of similar rocks

found   start or begin

goal   purpose

graduate   complete school

isolate   keep away from other people

lunar module   spacecraft designed to land on the Moon

NASA   National Astronautics and Space Administration, the agency that studies and carries out work in space

orbit   move or circle around something

procedure   method or plan

rendezvous   [RON • day • voo] joining together of two vehicles in space

retire   quit working at a particular job

simulator   model of a space vehicle used in training

More Books to Read

Aldrin, Buzz. *Reaching for the Moon*. New York: HarperCollins, 2005.

Crewe, Sabrina and Dale Anderson. *The First Moon Landing*. Milwaukee, Wis.: Gareth Stevens, 2004.

Hehner, Barbara. *First on the Moon*. New York: Hyperion/Madison, 1999.

Schyffert, Bea Uusma. *The Man Who Went to the Far Side of the Moon: The Story of* Apollo 11 *Astronaut Michael Collins*. San Francisco: Chronicle, 2003.

Places to Visit

Kids Space Place
1601 NASA Parkway (formerly NASA Road 1)
Houston, TX 77058
Visitor information: 281-244-2100

Kennedy Space Center
Mail Code DNPS
State Road 405
Kennedy Space Center, FL 32988
Visitor information: 321-449-4444

Index

32